# Contents

Ganges river dolphin

# Which 'horses' live in rivers?

The word 'hippopotamus' is Greek for 'river horse'. Hippos don't look much like horses really, but at dusk they do graze on river banks. Hippos have enormous mouths and huge teeth for pulling up and eating plants that grow at the water's edge.

Living in water keeps hippos cool in the African sun. Water makes them buoyant, so they half-float as they move, which saves energy. They are also fairly safe from land-living **predators** while they are in the water.

Hippopotamus

Big mouth

Large **canine** teeth

# Scary Creatures
## of the
# RIVER

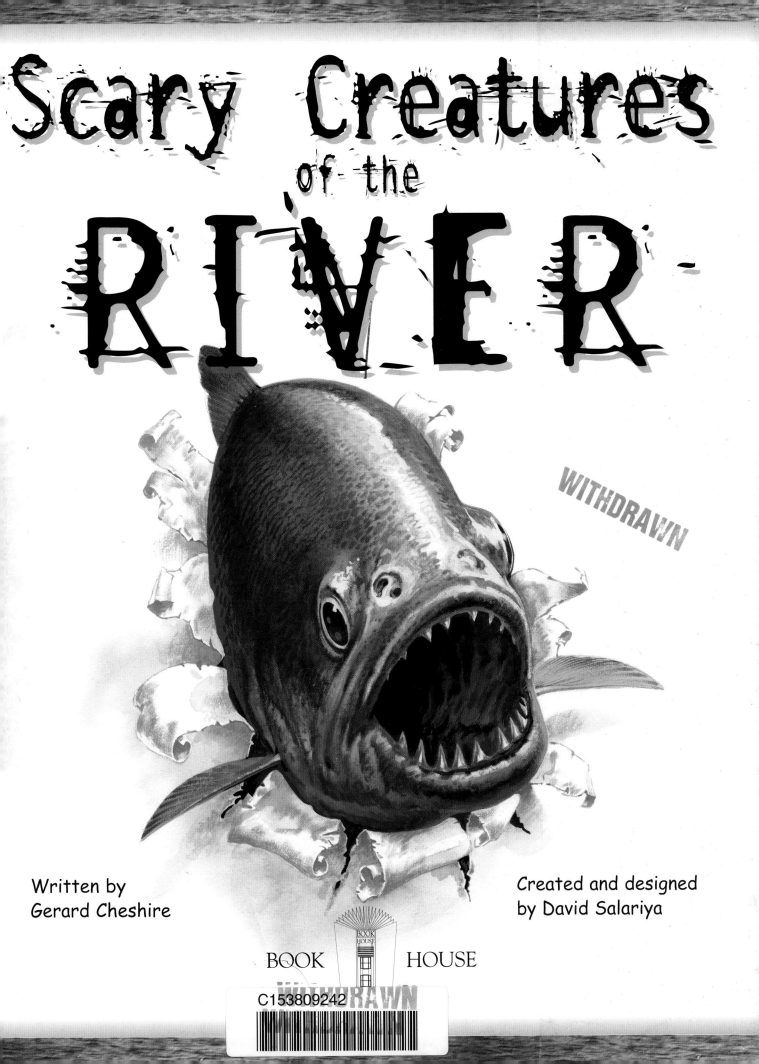

WITHDRAWN

Written by
Gerard Cheshire

Created and designed
by David Salariya

BOOK HOUSE

Author:

**Gerard Cheshire** has written many
books on natural history, and over the past
twelve years has cultivated an excellent
reputation as an author and editor. He lives in
Bath, England, with his wife and three sons.

Artists:

John Francis

Carolyn Scrace

Roger Hutchins

Series Creator:

**David Salariya** was born in Dundee,
Scotland. He established The Salariya Book Company
in 1989. He has illustrated a wide range of books and
has created many new series for publishers in the UK
and overseas. He lives in Brighton with his wife,
illustrator Shirley Willis, and their son.

Editorial Assistants:
Rob Walker, Tanya Kant

Picture Research:
Mark Bergin

Photo Credits:

t=top, b=bottom

fotolia: 5, 7, 10
Dreamstime: 22, 26, 27
iStockphoto: 8, 9, 18, 25
NHPA: 21

*Hippopotamus*

Published in Great Britain in 2009 by
Book House, an imprint of
**The Salariya Book Company Ltd**
25 Marlborough Place, Brighton BN1 1UB

SALARIYA

A catalogue record for this book is available
from the British Library.

HB ISBN: 978-1-906370-85-5
PB ISBN: 978-1-906370-86-2

Printed in China

Visit our website at **www.salariya.com**
for *free* electronic versions of:
**You Wouldn't Want to be an Egyptian Mummy!**
**You Wouldn't Want to be a Roman Gladiator!**
**Avoid Joining Shackleton's Polar Expedition!**
**Avoid Sailing on a 19th-Century Whaling Ship!**

PAPER FROM
SUSTAINABLE
**FORESTS**

## Did You Know?

A full-grown hippo can weigh as much as a family car – up to 3 tonnes.

## Are hippos scary creatures?

Hippos can become aggressive and charge if they feel threatened, or when they have young calves to protect. Many people are killed by them because they don't realise how dangerous hippos can be.

5

# Do monsters live in rivers?

People in many parts of the world tell stories about monsters living in rivers or lakes. Some of these stories may have been based on real animals. Catfish, for example, can grow monstrously large.

Manatees, dugongs and river dolphins are all **aquatic mammals** that sometimes get mistaken for monsters because of their size. Often they are glimpsed as they break the surface of the water to take a breath. People don't see them clearly, and allow their imagination to run riot.

Manatee

Ganges river dolphin

## Did You Know?

Manatees are slow-swimming, curious creatures. Many have been killed or wounded by swimming too close to boat propellers.

## Manatee

Manatees live in the sea much of the time, but they often swim into rivers during the winter. Dugongs are similar animals that live only in the sea.

# Can snakes hunt underwater?

Some snakes hunt for their **prey** in ponds and rivers. Grass snakes that live near water will eat frogs, newts and tadpoles, which are easy to swallow because they are soft and slippery. Grass snakes are very good swimmers, so they can easily chase their prey in the water.

The most fearsome river snake is the anaconda from South America, which can grow to around 10 metres long. It will eat just about anything that lives in rivers or comes to rivers to drink. Its large, forward-facing eyes help it to locate its prey and strike. Once caught, the victim is **constricted** (squeezed) until it dies of suffocation. The anaconda then swallows it whole.

Yellow anaconda

## Did You Know?

Anacondas can swallow animals as large as deer. Victims are grabbed from the water as they drink.

Yellow anaconda

# What is a 'living fossil'?

Some animals have hardly changed since prehistoric times. They are sometimes referred to as 'living **fossils**', because they are almost the same as ancient fossil animals. Crocodiles and alligators have not changed much in millions of years because they are perfectly adapted for their watery **habitat**.

Crocodiles like to hide their food underwater, so that other crocs can't find it.

X-Ray Vision

Hold the next page up to the light and see what's under the water.

See what's inside

Crocodile

**Crocodilians** include crocodiles, alligators, caimans and gavials (or gharials). They have lived on earth for about 145 million years.

Alligator

# What's the difference between crocodiles and alligators?

Crocodilians are very similar to one another, but there are slight differences. Alligators and crocodiles look virtually the same, but alligators have wider snouts and their lower teeth do not show when their mouths are shut. A crocodile's upper and lower teeth are always visible.

## Did You Know?

The temperature of the nest in which a crocodilian lays its eggs will determine whether the babies hatch as male or female.

Alligator

The eyes and nostrils of a crocodilian are on the top of its head. This allows the animal to see and breathe while its body remains hidden in the water.

Crocodilians have large claws on all four feet. They can haul themselves out of the water very quickly in pursuit of prey.

Crocodile

# Who said it's a fish-eat-fish world?

In all habitats, plants and animals form **food chains** or food webs. At the bottom of the food chain are plants, which are the primary food source. Small animals that eat the plants are themselves eaten by larger animals. Those larger animals, in turn, are eaten by even larger animals.

## What is the cycle of life?

The **cycle of life** is the entire process by which **nutrients** get passed from one living thing to another. When a **top predator** dies, the nutrients in its body return to the riverbed and the process begins all over again.

Stickleback

Tadpole

Algae

Small water plants called algae are eaten by water fleas and other tiny animals. The water fleas are then eaten by newts and tadpoles. Small fish such as sticklebacks then eat the newts and tadpoles.

# What is a top predator?

The largest predators of all are known as the top or super predators. But all plants and animals eventually die and are eaten by tiny living things known as **decomposers**. These recycle the nutrients that new plants and animals need to grow.

In any habitat the top predator is the largest predator, capable of eating all other animals. In some rivers, the top predator is the pike, which hunts and eats any other fish it can find. There are always fewer top predators than other animals, because they need the most food.

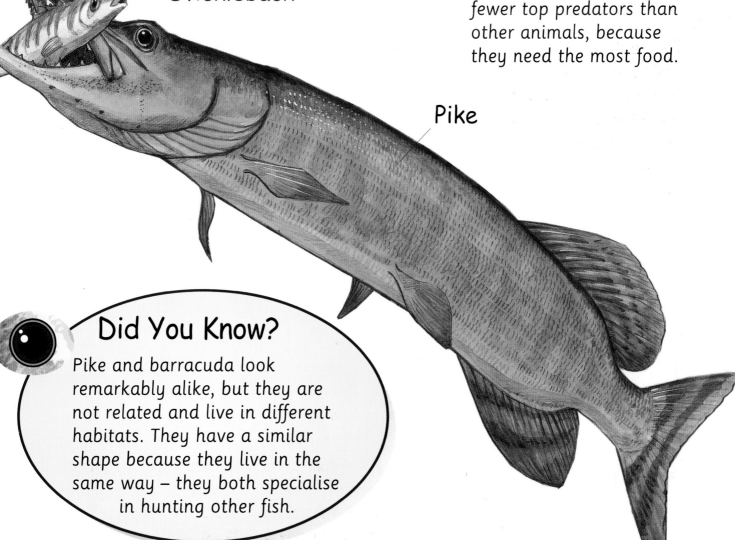

Stickleback

Pike

## Did You Know?

Pike and barracuda look remarkably alike, but they are not related and live in different habitats. They have a similar shape because they live in the same way – they both specialise in hunting other fish.

# How hard is it to survive?

For the many small animals that live in rivers, lakes and ponds, life is a constant struggle to avoid becoming prey to larger animals. There are so many different predators to avoid that small animals will be lucky to survive long enough to reproduce. Small creatures are often born in vast numbers, but only a few will make it to adulthood.

Pond skater

Great diving beetle

Tadpole

## Great diving beetle

Great diving beetles and their **larvae** are both skilled predators. They will attack and eat any aquatic animal that isn't too big to handle. They are especially fond of catching tadpoles, which are the young of frogs, toads and newts.

## Crayfish

Crayfish are small lobsters that live in **fresh water**. They are **scavengers**, eating scraps of food and any dead animals they find on the riverbed. They use their claws to grab food and hold it up to their mouths.

## Did You Know?

**Insects** that land on the surface of the water can be eaten by predators above and below. The pond skater is an insect that walks across the surface of the water looking for prey.

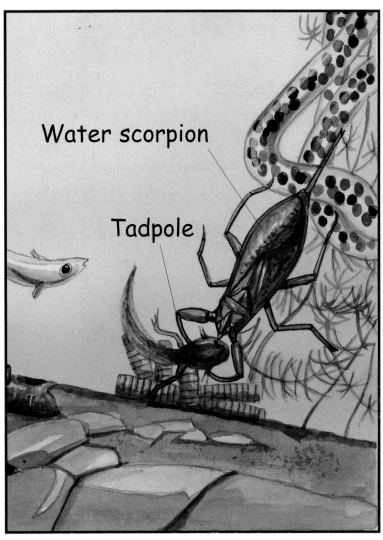

Water scorpion

Tadpole

## Water scorpion

The water scorpion uses its folding front legs to catch its prey, which it then consumes by sucking out the body fluids.

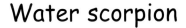

## Dragonfly nymph

A dragonfly larva (known as a **nymph**) has a folding lower jaw, which it shoots out to grab food.

## Water spider

The water spider has adapted to live underwater. It does not use its web for catching food, but for holding bubbles of air so that it can breathe. Its body hairs trap air, too.

# What makes piranhas so scary?

Piranhas are rather small fish, but they have a fearsome reputation. Unlike sharks, which may attack on their own, piranhas attack in groups. People have a natural fear of being attacked while swimming, because they cannot fight off a predator and swim at the same time. Thankfully, piranhas rarely attack humans.

**Piranha teeth**

A piranha's mouth is lined with razor-sharp teeth. They are designed to slice out chunks of flesh.

Shoal of piranhas

When they are not feeding, piranhas look harmless enough. They only become dangerous when they taste blood and go into a feeding frenzy.

## X-Ray Vision

Hold the page up to the light to see what happens to the alligator's hidden food store.

*See what's inside*

Alligator

Piranhas

Dead deer

19

Electric eel

Piranha

# How can fish be shocking?

Believe it or not, some fish can give an electric shock. The electric eel lives in murky water, where it is difficult to catch food. It shocks smaller fish, then eats them while they are stunned by the shock. The eels also use electric shocks to ward off larger predators.

The electric eel stores an electrical charge rather like an a charger in an electronic device. It releases an electric charge when it needs to stun its prey, and then quickly builds up a new charge.

Electric eel

The electric eel can give repeated electric shocks when under attack from predators. Most predators learn to stay away.

## Did You Know?

Electric rays, which live in saltwater habitats, also stun their prey with electric shocks.

# What is small but deadly?

Mosquitoes are certainly small but they can transmit deadly diseases when they suck blood. Malaria and yellow fever are spread in this way. These diseases can enter the human body when a mosquito plunges its needle-like mouth (**proboscis**) through the skin to feed on blood. It is thought that more people die from malaria than any other disease.

The mosquito carries the malaria infection from one person to another as it feeds. There have been attempts to control mosquito numbers, but they are very good at surviving.

A mosquito feeding

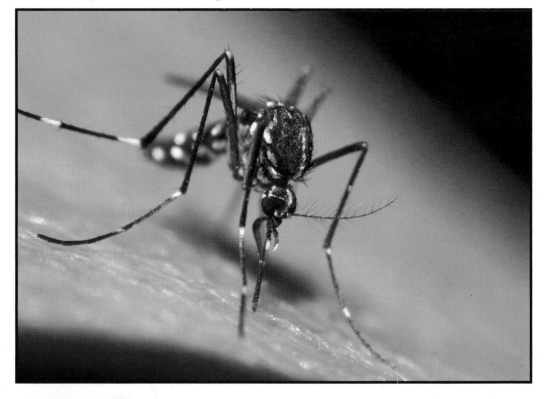

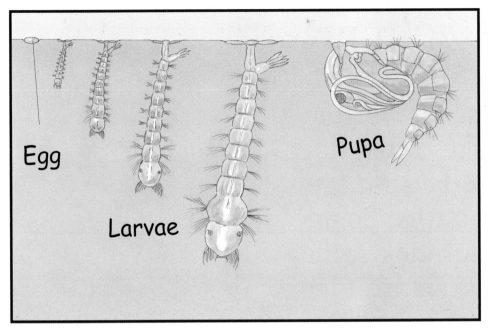

Egg

Larvae

Pupa

Mosquito larvae live in still water. They filter small particles of food and breathe air through their tails. The **pupae** float beneath the surface until they are ready to hatch into adult insects.

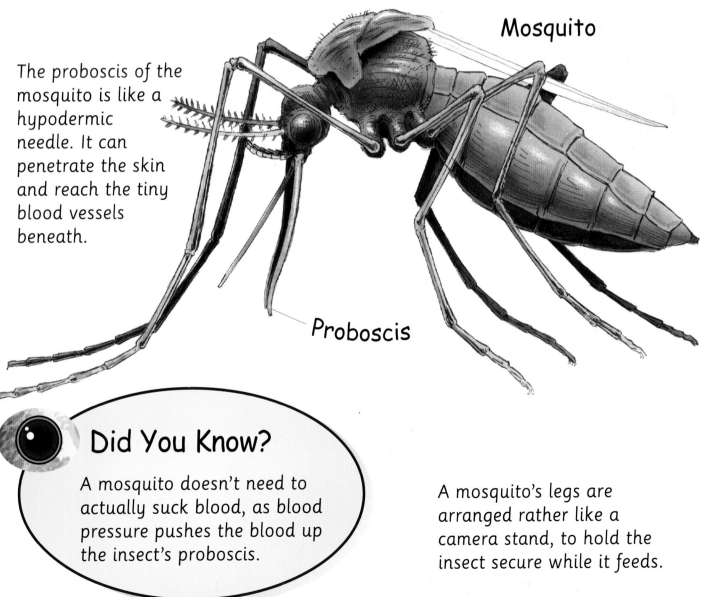

Mosquito

The proboscis of the mosquito is like a hypodermic needle. It can penetrate the skin and reach the tiny blood vessels beneath.

Proboscis

## Did You Know?

A mosquito doesn't need to actually suck blood, as blood pressure pushes the blood up the insect's proboscis.

A mosquito's legs are arranged rather like a camera stand, to hold the insect secure while it feeds.

# Do cats live in rivers?

Fish that feed at the bottom of rivers and lakes often have feelers called **barbels** on the sides of their mouths. Some have barbels that look rather like a cat's whiskers, so they are called 'catfish'. They use these barbels to feel things in the murky depths.

Catfish will eat anything they can find, including fish, frogs, birds and mammals.

## Did You Know?

Catfish eggs are often poisonous, so other fish don't eat them.

The Wels catfish, found in Europe and Asia, can grow to 2.5 metres long if it has enough space and enough food. Most catfish are smaller than this. They generally grow to the size that best suits their habitat.

# Catfish

Catfish have very wide mouths. They have teeth, but they feed by sucking in their prey and swallowing it whole, as snakes do.

The barbels on a catfish's head are rather like fingers. It uses them to sense its surroundings at the lake bottom, where it is too dark and murky to see anything.

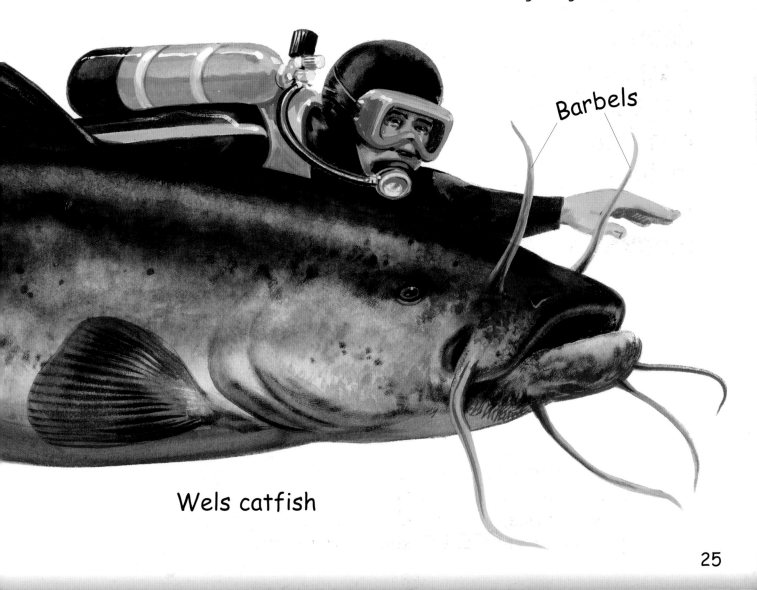

Barbels

Wels catfish

# Are there river aliens?

Up close, many of the minibeasts that live in rivers look so different from us that we might think of them as aliens from another world. The bodies of insects and other **invertebrates** are designed very differently from ours. When they are magnified, they look very scary indeed.

Dragonfly on a flower bud

 Did You Know?

Insects, spiders, crayfish and many other small animals have their skeletons on the outside of their bodies. They are known as **arthropods**.

Dragonflies have four large wings. They are very agile flyers, which enables them to chase and eat other flying insects. They catch them with their outstretched legs and munch them with their powerful jaws.

## Dragonfly

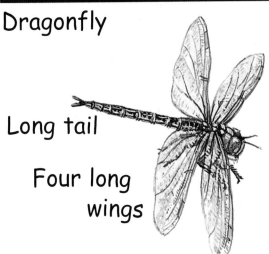

Long tail

Four long
wings

Dragonflies and damselflies have dome-shaped eyes. They can see all around them – in front, behind, below, above and to the sides. They can spot flying insects from any direction and quickly chase after them before they have time to escape.

# Where do scary river creatures live?

There are rivers all over the world, and they provide many different habitats for river creatures. Other freshwater habitats include streams, lakes, ponds, marshes and swamps.

North America

South America

## Alligator

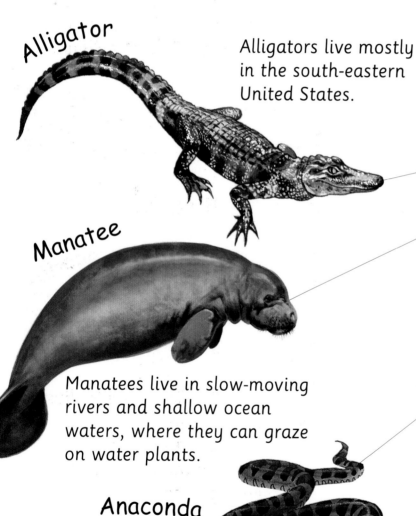

Alligators live mostly in the south-eastern United States.

## Manatee

Manatees live in slow-moving rivers and shallow ocean waters, where they can graze on water plants.

## Anaconda

Anacondas live along the **tributaries** of the great Amazon river in South America.

## Piranha

Piranhas also live in the tributaries of the Amazon. They can find their prey more easily in fairly still water.

# Hippopotamus

Hippos live in herds along the larger rivers of the African continent.

# Dragonfly

Dragonflies live all over the world. They are a familiar sight in Europe and North America.

Some giant catfish, which can grow to 3 metres long, live in the rivers of China.

## Giant catfish

## Indo-Pacific crocodile

Indo-Pacific crocodiles live in the rivers of Asia and northern Australia that run into the Indian and Pacific Oceans.

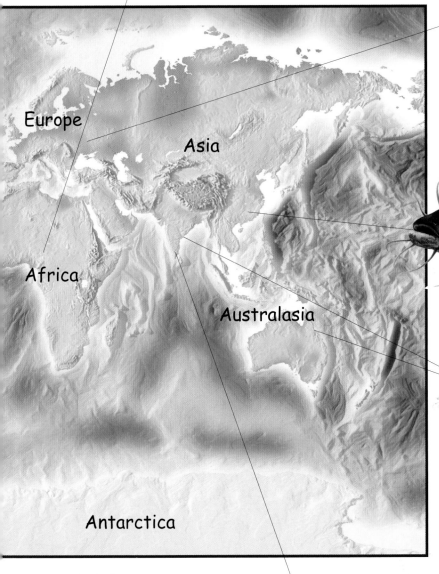

Europe

Asia

Africa

Australasia

Antarctica

River dolphins are rare creatures that live in the larger rivers of India and China.

## River dolphin

# River facts

The water in streams, rivers, lakes, ponds, marshes and swamps is described as 'fresh water', even though it may be stagnant and dirty. The water in seas and oceans is salt water. There are some animals that can live in both kinds of water, but most animals prefer to live in either fresh water or salt water all the time.

The place where a river meets the sea is called an estuary. The water in estuaries is a mixture of fresh water and salt water. It is described as 'brackish', which means that it is slightly salty.

Some species of fish, such as salmon and eels, are born in fresh water, grow to adulthood in salt water, and then move back to fresh water to breed. Salmon usually return to the river in which they were born. They may swim upstream for hundreds of kilometres to find a place to lay their eggs.

There are many different habitats in a river. Some animals live at the bottom of the river. They may lie on the bottom or burrow into the mud. Others live near the surface. Some animals stay in the middle of the river, while others live only along the banks. Many fish move to deeper water as they grow larger.

Animals that can move from land to water, or from water to land, are called **amphibious** or semi-aquatic. Frogs and toads are amphibious, but their young can live only in water. Some insects have larvae that can live only in water and adults that can live only on land.

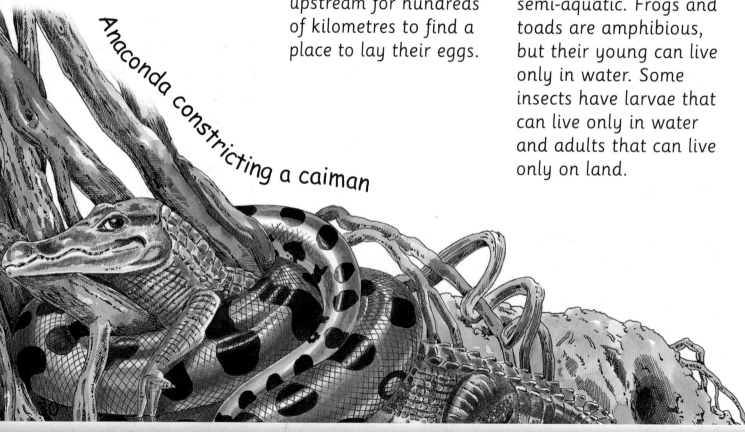

Anaconda constricting a caiman

# Glossary

**amphibious** Able to live in water and on land.

**aquatic** Living in water.

**arthropod** An animal that has its skeleton on the outside.

**barbel** A fleshy feeler growing from the face of some kinds of fish.

**canine teeth** The pointed teeth behind the front teeth of most mammals.

**constrict** To kill prey by squeezing it until it suffocates.

**crocodilians** Crocodiles and their relatives, such as alligators, caimans and gavials (or gharials).

**cycle of life** The process by which nutrients are passed from one living thing to another.

**decomposers** Tiny living things that break down the remains of dead plants and animals.

**food chain** The natural sequence of predator and prey.

**fossil** The remains of a dead animal or plant, preserved in the ground.

**fresh water** Any water that isn't salty.

**habitat** The place where an animal lives naturally.

**insect** An animal with six legs and a body in three sections: head, thorax, abdomen.

**invertebrate** An animal with no backbone.

**larva** (plural **larvae**) A young animal that will change into a different form when it becomes an adult.

**mammal** An animal that is born alive and then fed by its mother's milk.

**nutrients** Food or chemicals that a living thing needs in order to live and grow.

**nymph** A larva that turns into an adult insect without going into a pupa.

**predator** An animal that kills and eats other animals.

**prey** An animal hunted as food by a predator.

**proboscis** The long, sucking mouthparts of some insects.

**pupa** (plural **pupae**) The protective case inside which a larva turns into an adult insect.

**scavenger** An animal that eats dead matter, such as the leftover prey of other animals.

**top predator** (also called **super predator** or **apex predator**) A predator that is not preyed upon by any other animals.

**tributary** A river that flows into a larger river and becomes part of it.

# Index

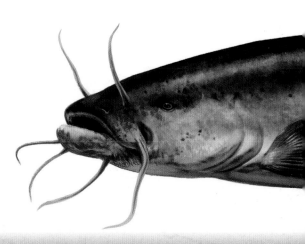